Copyright © 2018 by Montana Esco

Conversations Media Group

Brandon, MS 39042

All rights reserved. No part of this publication may be reproduced, stored in a retrieval system, or transmitted in any form or by any means (electronic, mechanical, photocopying or otherwise) without written permission from the author.

Written by Montana Esco with Cyrus Webb

Illustrated by C. A. Webb

Distributed by Conversations Media Group

Printed in the United States of America

Acknowledgements

First, thanks to God for allowing me this opportunity to share another important story of how to deal with bullies in our lives. Thanks to Cyrus Webb for your help in once again bringing Esco to life.

To my mother, father, kids, siblings and my friends who have supported me along the way and who purchased The Story of Esco, Thanks for believing in me.

Remember that we all rise together. Continue to Dream, Believe and Achieve.

~ Montana Esco

Esco enjoyed going to school.

He had his friends that he was able to play with and that were there for him when he needed them.

Everything was good for him until one day a new kid was introduced to his class. His name was Rick, and from the very first day Rick seemed to not like Esco at all.

You see Esco was smaller than most of the kids in his class, but it never bothered him until Rick made him feel almost invisible.

No matter how much Esco tried to avoid Rick, they seemed to always end up around each other, and then the insults would begin.

"Get out the way weirdo," Rick would say as they were walking down the hall.

"That's my seat shrimp!" Rick would yell at Esco in the cafeteria during lunch.

Esco looked for his friends to defend him or speak up for him when Rick was around, but they just put their heads down or looked away.

One day Esco was walking towards the school with his class project in hand, being very careful not to damage it on the way. Out of nowhere Rick appeared, running into Esco and knocking him down. His project was ruined!

"Watch where you're going, PeeWee," Rick said to Esco, not even stopping to see if Esco was okay.

Some of the kids laughed. Others looked at Esco, wanting to help but they ended up doing nothing.

That day Esco went home crying. He had done nothing to Rick, but every time they saw each other it seemed there was trouble.

"What's wrong, Esco," his mother asked him, seeing he was upset. He hadn't told her about all the things that had been happening with Rick, but now he couldn't hold it in any longer.

He told his mom about the way Rick picked on him, calling him names. He told her about his class project and how it had been ruined.

His teacher was going to allow him time to redo it, but Esco was upset that all of this was happening for no reason.

"I know it's hard, Esco," his mother said. "Especially when you haven't done anything to someone. Being mistreated is never fun, but let me share something with you that has helped me. The best way to make a friend is to be one."

"The best way to make a friend is to be one?" Esco repeated, thinking about what his mother said.

"That's right, Esco. Maybe this boy just needs a friend, someone that can show him that it's just nice to be nice."

That night Esco thought about what his mother said. The next day was Saturday, and he asked his mother if he could walk to the store with his friends to get some candy.

"Be careful," his mother said to him and his friends, and off they went.

As they were heading into the store Esco noticed that inside at the counter checking out was Rick!

'Oh no!' he thought to himself. 'Not again!' Then he thought about what his mother had said: The best way to make a friend is to be one.

Esco entered the store with his friends and he overheard Rick talking to the worker at the store. "I don't have $5," Rick was saying, counting the money he had pulled out of his pockets. "I only have $3.80."

The worker shook his head. "Then you will have to put something back," he told Rick. Rick looked at the things he was getting, trying to decide what he would have to do without.

At that moment Esco walked up to the counter, pulled out 2 $1 bills out of his pocket and handed them towards Rick. Rick had been so focused on trying to count his money that he hadn't noticed Esco and his friends coming into the store.

Looking at Esco handing him the $2 he couldn't believe the boy he had given such a hard time would do something like that. Rick reach out and took the money from Esco, said thank you and handed the money to the worker.

Esco turned around and saw his two friends starring at him with disbelief. When he joined them they asked why he did that for Rick, knowing how he had treated him. Esco shared what his mother had said to him about being a friend. He knew that if he was in a situation like that he would want someone to help him.

After Esco and his friends got what they wanted from the store they headed back towards his house. As they were walking they heard someone say "Hey! Esco!" Looking around they saw Rick!

They stopped, and Rick continued walking towards them.

When he got right in front of him Esco swallowed hard. What would he do now, Esco thought to himself.

"Why'd you do that for me, Esco?" Rick asked in probably the nicest voice that Esco had ever heard from him. "I'm always giving you trouble. What made you help me like that?"

Esco swallowed again. "I would want someone to do that for me if I was in need," he said to Rick. "Besides the best way to make a friend is to be one, right?"

Rick stared at him for a moment and then smiled. He smiled!

"That's right," he finally said to Esco. He stuck his hand out for Esco to shake it. "You're alright with me Esco."

Esco smiled, shook his hand and said "Thanks".

Rick turned around and walked away. Esco's friends looked at each other and then at Esco and said "Whoa".

On Monday Esco went to school feeling better. No matter what happened with Rick he was determined for it not to ruin his day. As he was walking towards the school with his class project out of nowhere once again appeared

Rick! Esco stopped at the door, waiting to see what would happen next.

To his surprise, Rick opened the door and nodded for Esco to go in! Esco nodded at Rick, walked into the school and breathed a sigh of relief.

After that he never had any problems out of Rick at school or anywhere. One day after school Esco was in the store buying some treats and as he walked towards the counter he noticed Rick walking into the store. The two spoke to each other and after the worked told Esco the total, Rick pulled money out of his pocket and paid for Esco's things!

"I owe you," Rick told Esco. Esco said thank you and walked out of the store.

His mom was right. The way to make friends is to be one, and he had made a friend with Rick.

Do you remember?

1. Esco liked school, but what was the name of the bully?
2. What were some of the things that the bully did to Esco?
3. What did Esco's mom tell him to do?
4. When at the store how did Esco get a chance to do what his mom told him?
5. What happened with Esco and the bully after that?
6. Have you had to deal with a bully?
7. How can you use the advice of Esco's mom?

Also by Montana Esco

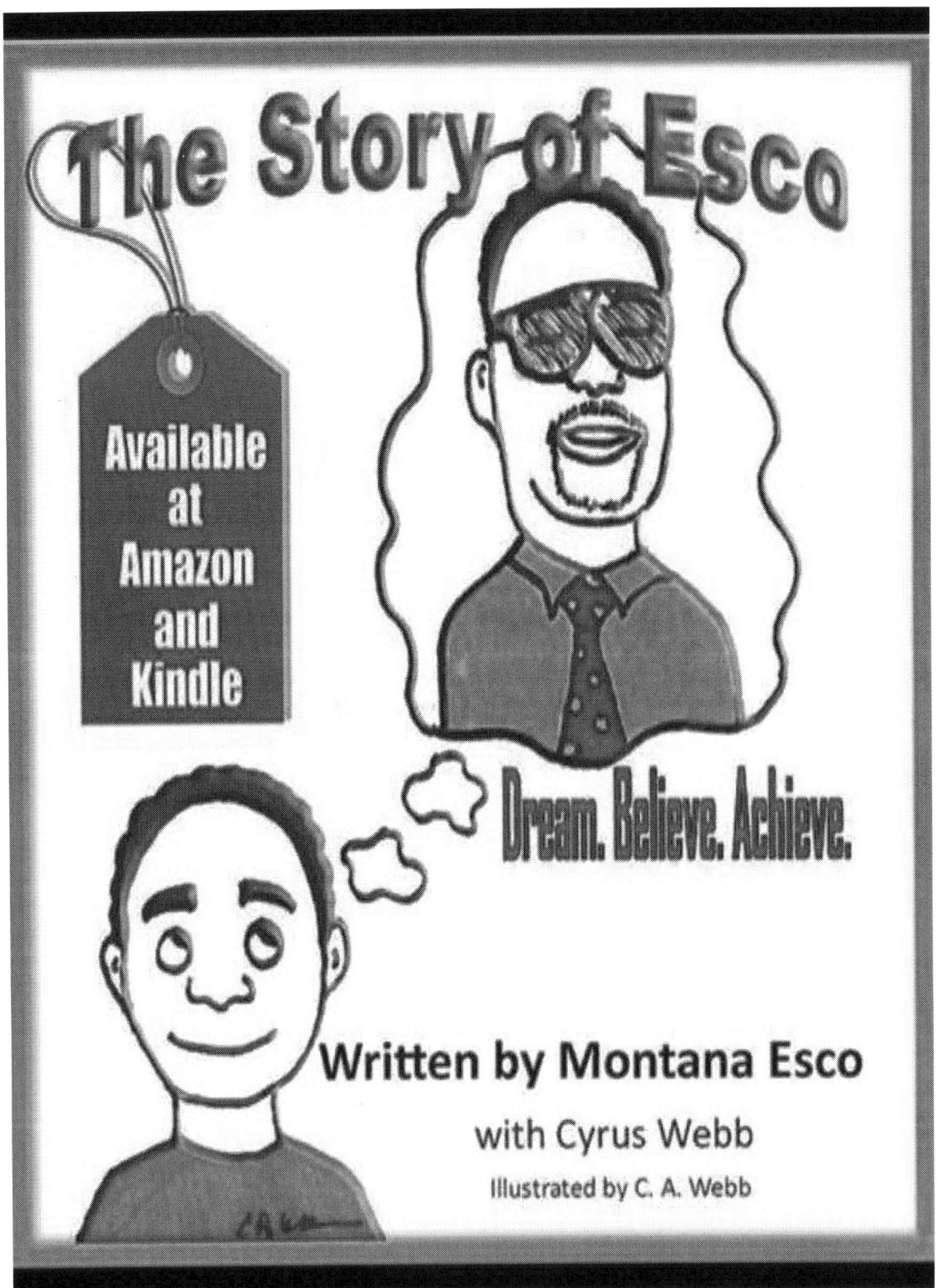